DAVEY
& THE DRAGON FEATHER

DAVEY & THE DRAGON FEATHER

Book 1: Adam and Eve;
Noah's Ark; Joseph and His Coat of Many Colors;
Moses, Prince of Egypt

Published by Delcie Palmer
Copyright © 2024 by Delcie Palmer
Unless otherwise indicated, all scripture quotations are taken from the New King James Version®. Copyright © 1982 by Thomas Nelson. Used by permission. All rights reserved.
Scripture taken from the Holy Bible, New International Version®. NIV®. Copyright © 1973, 1978, 1984 by International Bible Society. Used by permission of Zondervan. All rights reserved worldwide.
All rights reserved, including the right to reproduce this book or portions thereof in any form whatsoever.
For information, bulk purchases, or discounts, address faithbridgecafe.com
NO AI TRAINING: Use of this publication to train generative AI is expressly prohibited.

ISBN: 978-1-7324742-1-5

Davey & the Dragon Feather

Davey's Birthday Surprise

"I'm not an airplane, Dad, not a kite. Pleeease slow down." Dad was holding onto my hand and running down the street! He was going so fast, I could barely keep my feet on the ground. Finally he stopped and knelt down in front of me. He seemed so tall, then all of a sudden, there he was on my level. I could see some sweat over his left eyebrow, and he squinted to keep it from draining into his eyes.

"Davey," he said, while brushing some dust from my T-shirt. "This is your special day, but you won't get the surprise I have for you if we don't hurry." Then, he sprang to his feet like a big kangaroo, and started walking really fast, nearly running again. "Whoa," I said. "Super whoa, whoa, whoa!" And we both started laughing as my feet nearly lifted off the ground.

At the very next corner we saw a big bus with bright headlights racing down the street. Dad let go of my hand and started jumping up and down and up and down. He waved at the bus and then he put his fingers inside his lips and gave a very loud whistle sound, but the bus just drove by us.

"He didn't see us, Dad," I said.

"How is it he didn't see us? Didn't he see me waving?" He sounded angry. "Hurry, Davey."

"Dad, can we stop for baklava?" I asked as we ran by a bakery.

"No, Davey, no baklava. Hurry, hurry." Then, he lifted me up and swung me onto his back like a book bag. I hung onto his shoulders as he kept running, and suddenly it began to rain. Slosh, slosh, slosh; I could hear his heavy shoes slapping the water and mud.

"I'm getting wet." I squinted so that I could see through the water rolling down my forehead. Then a street light came on to my right, then another one, and another one, like lights at Christmas time, lighting up the narrow street that leads to the center of the city.

I've lived here all my life, yet Jerusalem is always so awesome to me. I can see the Wailing Wall where I prayed for my cousin when she went away to college in America. And I can see the golden Dome on the Temple Mount. And all the trees smell like almonds when it rains.

"No worries, Davey," Dad said, as he hurried around a corner. "We're almost there."

Finally, we saw the building—a small red house with lots and lots of windows, sitting right in the middle of downtown Jerusalem. It had a red awning in front and a pink stone walkway leading to the door.

"This is Uncle Heim's coffee shop!" I said.

"That's right, Davey," Dad said. "The Faith-Bridge Café."

"Faith-Bridge. They have baklava," I reminded him.

Before we went inside, Dad slowed down and knelt in front of me. "Now, Davey, your Uncle Heim is waiting for us inside. He leaves today for Egypt, but I think we made it in time. He has a special present for your birthday."

"Whoa, a present for me?!" I almost forgot about the rain.

"Yes. I see his car, so I think he is still here. Come on." And we hurried inside the café, and there was Uncle Heim standing at the register. He smiled a large smile when he saw me, and he rubbed his big tummy and laughed out loud.

"Oh, who is that big boy with you, Louie?" he asked Dad. "Did you find him outside? Is he following you around?"

"It's me, Davey," I said laughing.

"Oh, Davey. You are a big boy. I didn't recognize you. Okay, you two, sit down, sit down at the counter."

"We ran in the rain. I thank God you are still here," Dad said, as he pulled out a chair for me to sit on.

"You almost missed me. I was about to go to the airport. Well, since you are here, Davey, I have a special surprise and in one million and twenty years, you would never guess what it is." Uncle was reaching under the counter while watching my eyes. Then, he lifted a long piece of white wrapping paper and rested it on the counter in front of me. "Well ," he said, "don't just sit there Davey! Open it."

I pulled the paper away and wow, wow, wow. "Whoa!" I said. "It's, it's..."

"A dragon feather!" Uncle's eyes were wide like saucers, and he smiled the biggest smile I had ever seen.

"Whoa!" I said. "Where did you get it?" I lifted it up and ran my hand along the length of the feather which seemed to go and on and on. "It's awesome."

"I found it in a cave outside Tel Aviv. Do you like it?" asked Uncle Heim.

I could tell the feather was very old, but also the prettiest I had ever seen. "I love it, Uncle Heim."

"You should have seen it before I dusted off all the dirt," he said.

"Whoa," I said.

"Well, it's yours."

"Mine?"

"Yours. It's a feather from the ancient dragon bird. The bird that probably existed in the time of Noah, and in the time of the Garden of Eden. It's called Archaeopteryx. A red dinosaur bird."

"Archapele?" I asked.

"Never mind, Davey," said Uncle Heim. "You will learn how to pronounce it later. Just remember, it's probably the last one on Earth. So you must take care of it."

"Happy birthday, Davey," Dad said, smiling. "What do you say to Uncle Heim? He is giving you a very special present."

"Thank you, Uncle Heim. I promise to take care of it." And I gave him a hug. "A dinosaur bird," I said while looking at the different shades of red in the feather. "It lived a long time ago."

"Yes, indeed," said Uncle Heim. "And Davey, you are a bright boy in school! In the fifth grade now?"

"My teacher said I read and write like I am in the tenth grade." Dad smiled and rubbed the top of my head.

"Davey, do you know why you are given that feather for your birthday?" Dad asked. I shook my head. "Because you are going to tell our story," he said.

"Tell our story?" I asked.

"Yes. The story of our ancestors; the Bible stories."

"With a feather?" I asked.

"Look closely, Davey," said Uncle Heim. "It has ink. Lots and lots of ink. See here." And he showed me that the tip of the feather had an opening, and indeed, it was filled with black ink.

"You have a good mind, Davey," Dad said. "You are the one to tell our story using that special writing feather. It has ink, and now all you need is paper and that smart mind of yours. Remember too, you won't be alone. God is always with you. He is very powerful, and kind, and He will help you if you ask Him."

"He's the most important part," said Uncle Heim.

"Writing with the feather would be awesome!" I said. "Look at how it shines in the light. Is it a magic feather?"

"No," Dad said. "It doesn't have any magical powers. Davey, if you take this challenge we are giving you, then I am confident you can do it with God's help. There won't be any shortcuts or magic. You might have to watch less television, and maybe you don't need to play as many video games."

"Davey," said Uncle Heim, "either way, the feather is yours. The question is, how will you use it?"

"Hmmm. This is the most awesome feather I've ever seen; so maybe I don't need the video games. Maybe I don't need so much television. And I love my family and want to tell our story." I nodded. "I will use it to write our story." And everyone smiled. "I will write in my spare time. At my desk, at the beach, at the park...I will take the dragon feather with me wherever I go, until I am finished writing our stories. But where do I begin?"

"At the beginning, of course," Dad said, smiling. "Tell the whole story, Davey, from the book of Genesis all the way up to now. Use what you remember from Bible studies; and try to imagine how it was back in those days."

* * * * * * *

That night in my room, I wanted to try out the Dragon feather so I sat at my desk and reached for a piece of paper. Then, I asked Father God to help me. I wanted Him to be with me when I began writing and all the way to the end. So, I closed my eyes and said:

> Father God in Heaven, You are awesome! I really like
> all the stuff You do, like all the places You created.
> Thanks for food like humus, and pumpkins.
> Thanks, too, for blueberry ice-cream.
> Thanks for walnuts, lettuce, and figs.
>
> Now, Father God, please help me, because
> what happened was that my uncle gave me

a dragon feather for my birthday, and he
and my Dad kind of want me to use it to
write Bible Stories.

I really want to, but I don't know how
to start. I don't know all the words to use,
but You do, Father God. So, please help me
to use all the right words.

Dad said that whenever I ask You for
something, I should find some scripture to
stand on. So, I am standing on James 1:5-8
that says that you will give wisdom to
anybody who asks, even kids like me.
So, I'm believing you're gonna help me.
Thank You!

Whoa! I almost forgot. Guess what. I found
frogs in the pond near my school. It was
awesome!

    When I was done praying, I tested the Dragon feather. I made big swirly lines, and lots of loops, and wow, it works all right. It's just like writing with a regular pen or pencil. But I still don't know how to start the Bible stories.
    I am sure God heard me when I prayed, so I am just going to trust Him to help me figure it out. "Father, God, what was it like when You created the world?" I thought about what I read in the Bible, in the book of Genesis, when God created the heavens and the earth. Then, I place the tip of the feather on paper and try to imagine those first days of creation. I close my eyes, and Whoa!!
    Bam, Kapowey, Kachowey!! I see lighting, then I see planet Earth. The whole planet is a blob, no life anywhere, and it's totally dark here; but all that is about to change.
    The Spirit of God is hovering above the planet!

GENESIS

Bam, Kapowey, Kachowey, and "God said, 'Let there be light.'"[1] And whoa! He's like a supernova! I mean, wow! He's all energy and power and His voice is awesome, like thunder and rain, and warm all at once!

Kapowey!! And there was light, just as God said. And then God said, "Let the waters under the heavens be gathered together in one place..."[2] And then I saw, swoosh, swoosh, large oceans rising up all across the planet, and large waves crashing. And then I can see super large sea turtles, and whales, and anemones, along with white dolphins, and pink corals and all sorts of star fish; He created them all.

"So God created great sea creatures and every living thing that moves...and every winged bird according to its kind. And God saw that it was good."[3] And it's the prettiest thing I ever saw. And I even think I see a dragon bird, with long red feathers, flying low over a mountain top. Squaak!! Squaak!! That's the sound it makes.

And God looked across His creation and saw that it was good. And wow, it really was good! I don't know how He did it, but Kachowey! His words brought into being a large group of trees rolling up from the Earth; mountains sprung up and it was wild with green grass, and I can hear birds singing and it's super awesome. God is awesome! And I want to be like Him when I grow up.

And so God made this really cool creation: A whole planet full of creatures and green trees. And I can see, like from a mountain top and looking across the valleys, that it's peaceful and light is bouncing off the trees. And it's quiet. And God is looking across His creation. But He's not finished creating. He has one more thing He wants to do. This one is very special. He will create mankind. He will create the first man and woman, and they will have kids until many years later, I am born, and you are born.

Then God said, "Let us make man in Our image, according to Our likeness..."[4] And God made man in His image. He didn't make man to look like the elephant or the rhinoceros. He didn't make man to look like the great whale or the sea eagle. No. He created man to look like Himself. He created man in His own image, with legs and toes and eyebrows.

"So God created man in His image; in the image of God He created him; male and female He created them. Then God blessed them, and said to them, 'Be fruitful and multiply; fill the earth and subdue it, have dominion over the fish of the sea, over the birds of the air, and over every living thing that moves on the earth.'"[5]

Okay, OK, so now I see. God created mankind, my ancestors and your ancestors, for a special reason. And at least part of the reason is so that we could have dominion over the Earth. Wow. Do-min-ion. What does that mean? It simply means to have control over something. If you own a bicycle then you have do-min-ion over the bicycle. That means you have control over it and ought to take care of it.

So God gave people dominion over the Earth, so they should take care of the sea horse and the great whale, potato plants, and each other. They should build buildings, be fruitful and multiply. Just grow and grow and grow. The Earth, with all the trees, sunlight, and apples, is a gift from God; a very, very special blessing. We all have the job of taking care of the Earth and making sure it's okay. So God the King created the heavens and Earth for you and for me, and for all the fish in the sea, because He loves us.

And that's the story of how our world began.

ADAM AND EVE

I live in the Old City of Jerusalem; that's the part of the City with the Wailing Wall. The Wall is super special because it used to be part of God's holy temple. Sometimes Dad takes me there to pray. The Wall is only a ten-minute walk from our house.

We have a small house, but Dad was lucky, he said, because he got it with nearly an acre of land. And wow, guess what. He built a solarium in the backyard; that's a long glass house for trees and birds.

The solarium has some of the stuff I got for my birthday. When I turned five years old, Dad surprised me with a nutchack bird. That's a bird that stands upside down underneath tree limbs and search for insects. I call him Bones because he's super skinny. I never saw such a skinny bird. And he looks so funny hanging upside down. So, I like going into the solarium and hanging out with Bones and the other animals. We have a calico cat—that's a cat without any hair on it. And it sure looks funny. And we also have a llama, a real live llama from Peru. And we have, too, a goat named Sam.

The solarium is lots of fun, and my parents made it for me because of how much they love me. So today I am writing with the dragon feather while I sit on my bicycle in the solarium. I want to write about the Garden of Eden; that special place God made for Adam and Eve because He loves them so much.

Dad said to use my imagination when I write the Bible stories; to try to imagine what it was like back in those days. So I close my eyes, and whoa!

I see the Garden of Eden. I can see it in my mind, like I'm actually there. The Garden has pretty trees and it has fresh water running through it, and the trees don't look like the trees from my solarium; the trees in the Garden are magical trees. And in the center of the Garden is a special tree called the Tree of the Knowledge of Good and Evil.[6] I'll call it, "the tree of knowledge," for short.

And I see two people walking around. That must be Adam and Eve. And Someone else is there. God is there; God the King of the Garden, and King of the whole entire world; and I can tell it's Him because my heart feels warm inside. He's teaching Adam and Eve how to live in the Garden. They can eat from any

tree in the Garden, He tells them, but they must not eat from the tree of knowledge because they would die. So, it's not food like with the other trees.

Oh wow, what's that? It's a snake[7] walking around on skinny legs. That's lucifer, the devil; the lord of the flies. And he keeps looking over at Eve. I want to tell her to run away from him; he's really creepy. But I can't tell her, and there he goes walking over to her; he wants her to eat from the tree of knowledge.[8] If she eats from the tree of knowledge, she would learn about good stuff like God's love, hot chocolate and hugs. But she would also learn about evil stuff, like the devil, and broken toes, and people dying. That's why lucifer wants her to eat from the tree; so she can know evil and be scared and sad.

Adam and Eve were made to live forever in that really cool Garden and have dominion over the Earth. They weren't supposed to die, but the devil tricks them. So Eve picks the fruit from the tree of knowledge, takes a bite and gives some of it to Adam, and Adam also ate.[9]

At that moment, something changes. They now know evil. They know fear, and worry, and trouble. They look over at the devil and they can see why God didn't want them to eat from the tree. They see that lucifer wants to kill them; he wants them to die; he hates God and he hates them, too.

And he is not going to leave them alone after this, but will trouble them a lot. Now, it gets really sad because they are scared and they hide in the trees. And God is sad too, because he never wanted them to be afraid. So, He goes looking for them and when he finds them hiding, they tell Him what they did.[10]

To keep Adam and Eve from making things worse, God puts them outside the Garden. And now they have to work for a living. Things don't grow so easy outside the Garden as it does in the Garden, so they have to figure out how to farm and raise animals and get along. So, yeah, that story is kind of sad. I wish they listened to God; He was just trying to keep them safe.

The devil isn't going to just get away with all he did to Adam and Eve. The Bible calls him a liar and the father of lies. After he lied to Adam and Eve, he lost his legs, and he has to slither on the ground.[11] One day, God will put an end to him. It's a long time away from those days, but one day, one of Adam's kids will crush lucifer's head.[12] That's what it says in the Bible.

That's the story of Adam and Eve and how all of mankind began. They were the first man and woman. We are all from Adam and Eve, and so as I tell the Bible stories, I am telling my family's story, and your story, too!!

...NOAH'S ARK....

NOAH'S ARK

So, there is this place downtown Jerusalem that sells humus and pita bread, and it has a horse carousel out front, and for a couple of shekels (that's around 20 cents), I can ride on the carousel for five minutes. One day, Dad was inside buying lunch when I figured I'd try it out. So, I dropped in a few shekels and sat on the blue horse.

Then, one of the big kids from my school came along and jumped on the black horse; and he sat on the horse backwards, and kept making ugly faces at me. And he tried to slow down the ride by dragging his feet on the ground. I kept telling him to stop and so when he didn't, I jumped off the horse and I was about to clobber him when Dad came out the store and saw me.

"Davey!" He said. And I got in trouble for nearly getting into a fight. "It's a tough world, Davey," Dad said, as we were walking home. "Pick your battles. A carousel ride is not worth fighting over." I guess he's right, but it still made me mad.

I know what it feels like to get pushed around just 'cause I'm not as big as the big boys from school. I feel pretty bad when they try to push me around. And one of the kids even brought drugs to school. Dad said the world is not what it used to be; that it's going downhill.

I told that story because I think I know how Noah felt. That's the next Bible story. I say Bible story, but it actually happened; maybe not exactly how I tell it, but I think I come pretty close.

So, I'm sitting at my desk with the dragon feather and my doggies Chocolate Chip, and Mocha, are lounging around me. (I gave them those names 'cause they sort of have colors like ice cream.) I'm imagining how it was back in the days of Noah, and trying to remember what I learned in Bible class. I reach for the dragon feather, and I pray because God helps me. Then, I close my eyes.

I see an Ark, and heavy rain. Noah is in the Ark with his family and lots of animals. So, what's going on here?

It all started the day God told Noah to build an ark because He was going to send a great flood to wash away all the people on Earth. But why would God do that? Because everybody did bad stuff. They were really mean and kept killing each other, stealing, and lying. God wanted to help them, but they wouldn't listen.

God is a Dad. He loves all His creation. But at that time in history, people did bad all the time. And it made Him sad. But Noah was different from all the other people. Here it is from the Bible:

"Then the Lord saw that the wickedness of man was great in the earth, and… (their) heart was only evil continually. And the Lord was sorry that He had man on the earth, and He was grieved in His heart. So the Lord said, 'I will destroy man whom I have created from the face of the earth, both man and beast, creeping thing and birds of the air, for I am sorry that I have made them.' But Noah found grace in the eyes of the Lord.'"[13]

So God will send a flood, but He will save Noah and his family. In order to be safe, Noah has to build the Ark and get everyone inside before the flood comes!

God said to Noah, "I am going to put an end to all people, for the earth is filled with violence because of them... So make yourself an ark of cypress wood; make rooms in it and coat it with pitch inside and out... You are to bring into the arc two of all living creatures, male and female, to keep them alive with you."[14]

So, God told Noah to build the Ark of cypress wood, and to take some of the animals inside, and close the doors because it would rain for forty days and forty nights. Noah did just as God said, and then it started to rain. For forty days and forty nights, it rained and rained until all the Earth was covered with water. After forty days, the water on the land dried up, and Noah opened the window of the Ark.

Noah must have been super happy to get off the Ark. And then God spoke to him about what happened. He didn't want Noah to worry about another flood so He promised him that He would never again send a flood to destroy the Earth. And, just so Noah and his family would remember the promise, He set a sign in the Heavens: a colorful rainbow!!

"Then God spoke to Noah and to his sons with him, saying...' Behold I establish My covenant with you and your descendants after you… never again shall there be a flood to destroy the earth.'"[15]

"And God said: 'This is the sign of the covenant which I make between Me and you, and every living creature that is with you, for perpetual generations: I set My rainbow in the cloud, and it shall be for the sign of the covenant between Me and the earth.'"[16]

So you see, God made a promise to Noah and even a promise to the Earth and all the living creatures He created that He would not send another flood like that one. He didn't want to send it in the first place, but sin was so bad that He decided to wash it all away. Noah and His family, and some of the animals, would be the ones to start over on clean Earth. And God didn't want Noah to be nervous about more rain, so He promised him that there would be no more floods like that one, and He made a sign in the clouds—a rainbow, a really pretty rainbow.

And that's how it was in the days of Noah.

JOSEPH and His Coat of Many Colors

Every time I have a birthday, Dad does something special for me. When I was five, Dad built the solarium in our back yard. I got the llama goat when I was seven, and the nutchack bird when I turned eight years old. This year, when I turned twelve, I got the Dragon feather. I get lots of cool things, so I am always happy when it comes time for my birthday.

I have four brothers. I am the youngest, and I think that's why Dad always does something special for my birthday. One day, I took some of my new toys to show to my brothers, and my oldest brother, Eli, took my toy truck and pulled the wheels off and then he pulled off the hood and stepped on it. I felt real sad and so I started to cry and all my brothers started laughing at me and called me, "baby Davey." Dad says they're just jealous, but it made me really sad.

When I read the story about Joseph in the Bible, I totally know how he felt. His brothers didn't like him, either. So, I totally get how he feels. That's our next Bible story. It's about Joseph, a guy a little older than me who lived near Jerusalem, not too far from where I live now. But his story took place a long time ago, back in Bible days.

I pray to God to help me imagine what it was like back in the days of Joseph. Then, I see dust, lots of sand, and a large Camel standing in the shade of olives trees. And I see Joseph. He's standing outside his Dad's tent and showing his brothers his new birthday gift: an awesome colorful robe. The colors of the robe look like the colors of the rainbow.

****

Joseph was really happy that his Dad loved him so much, and that he made that special robe for him, but his brothers were jealous. They really hated Joseph. What happens next will make them hate him even more.

One night while Joseph was sleeping, he dreamt that he saw the sky; then, something surprising happened. He saw the moon and the sun and eleven stars bowing down to him. Wow. The sun and the moon and eleven stars were bowing down to Joseph? That's pretty amazing, right? But what does it mean? God was using the dream to show Joseph the future.

The big moon, the hot sun, and eleven stars all bowed down to Joseph the way his family would one day bow down to him. God was telling Joseph that one day he would become a very important person, and his family would show him honor by bowing to him. That's a very special dream. But when Joseph told his brothers about the dream, they hated him even more. They didn't believe they would ever bow down to Joseph.

It must have been very hard for Joseph to be around his brothers, knowing that they hated him. Maybe he wondered, "How can I get these guys to like me? Look at them; they look so mean."

One day Joseph's dad sent him to a place called Shechem to check on his brothers. When his brothers saw him coming, they came up with a plan to get rid of him. They said, "Let's kill him and throw him into one of these cisterns and say that a ferocious animal devoured him. Then we will see what comes of his dreams."[17] Oh no, they're going to throw Joseph into a pit. As I'm writing this, my doggie, Mocha, starts to bark. Maybe he sees it too; Joseph is in trouble!

When Joseph walked up to his brothers, he probably knew something was wrong by the mean way they looked at him. Suddenly, they grabbed him, tore off his pretty coat, and threw him into a pit. Then, they went to have lunch as if nothing happened.

Joseph must have been frightened, and felt alone. But, God could see everything, and had a plan to rescue him! While the brothers were eating, a caravan, a group of men traveling together, came by with their camels and spices and herbs. These were the Ishmaelites from a place called Gilead. And wow, their camels were loaded with spices and stuff, and they were heading to Egypt.

Joseph's brothers decided that instead of killing him, they would sell him to the Ishamelite merchants. So, they pulled him from the dusty pit and sold him for twenty sheckels of silver, and the Ishmaelites carried him off to Egypt as a slave.

Joseph didn't know when he'd ever see his Dad again, or what would happen to him once he got to Egypt. Would he end up in a Roman coliseum as a gladiator? Would he have to fight a ferocious lion? Would he be able to escape and get back home to Jacob, his father? He simply had to trust God with his future!

Meanwhile, back in the field in Shechem, the evil brothers came up with a plan to dip Joseph's robe in animal blood and take it to Jacob and pretend that a wild animal killed him. They probably put on a sad face when they walked up to Jacob with the robe. "It is my son's robe!" Jacob said when he saw Joseph's torn up and bloody robe. "Joseph has surely been torn to pieces." And how Jacob must have wept for Joseph. He had no idea that Joseph was not torn to pieces, but was sold by his evil brothers to the Ishmaelite merchants.

And wow! When Joseph got to Egypt, what did he see? He saw lots of sand, and pyramids in the hot sun; and he saw Cairo, the capital city, with tall buildings, and he must have seen horses, and a marketplace selling pita bread and humus; and there were probably even camels, and chariots for the soldiers to ride in with their shiny helmets, and children playing. But more than anything, I am sure, he wanted to see his Dad.

* * * * * * *

In the time Joseph lived, Pharaoh was king of Egypt, and people were brought and sold like cows and horses. And so, since Joseph was a slave, he was sold to a wealthy man called Potipher, one of the soldiers in Pharaoh's army. Was Joseph afraid? Was he crying? He must have been nervous about his new home. But all the while, the Lord was with Joseph. God never left Joseph alone. Even though Joseph couldn't see Him, He was him in Spirit.

Joseph decided to do his very best even though he was a slave, and he was such a hard worker that Potipher put him in charge of his entire household. He was in charge of all the food, including wheat, couscous, and figs. He was in charge of corn and any type of bird or pheasant or foul. He was in charge of eggs, berries, melons, and potato plants, carrots, pumpkins, and rye. He was in charge of everything that Potipher owned.

But in all his good work, he faced one big problem. Potipher's wife wouldn't leave him alone; she kept trying to give him hugs and kisses and stuff. But she already had a husband, so Joseph knew to stay away from her.

One day when Potipher was away and all the other servants were outside, Potipher's wife tried again to tempt him, but Joseph was very smart and ran away; but as he was running away, she grabbed onto his coat.

He left the coat in her hands and ran out the room. Phew! That was close! Then, because she was evil, she yelled for help and when the servants came inside, she said Joseph tried to take advantage of her. When her husband, Potipher, came home, she told him the same crazy story, and Potipher had Joseph thrown into prison.[20]

Whoa! Joseph is in prison! But what about the dream he had about his brothers bowing down to him? What about the future God has for him? Is this how his story ends, with him locked away? This is the great part about this story; no matter how bad things got, God never left Joseph. He stayed with him, and worked it all out, somehow.

The Bible says, "While Joseph was in prison, the Lord was with him; He showed him kindness and granted him favor..."[21] So you see, God really took good care of him.

Not only that, God gave Joseph a super-power! With God's help, Joseph could interpret dreams. That's awesome. He could tell people the meaning of their dreams, and that's going to be really helpful in the days ahead.

When the other prisoners found out that Joseph could interpret dreams, they started going to him for help. Hey Joseph, help us out.

One guy used to be Pharaoh's cup bearer, but something went wrong and Pharaoh had him thrown into prison. He dreamt that he saw himself giving Pharaoh a drink. So what's all that about? Joseph told him it meant that he would get his old job back working for Pharaoh as a cup bearer. He was super happy to hear that! No more prison food!!

Then some other guy who used to be Pharaoh's baker told Joseph about a dream he had; he dreamt about birds eating bread from a basket on his head. But what does it mean? Joseph told him it meant he would lose his head; he would be killed. Sadly for that guy, it happened just as Joseph said.

Eventually, the cup bearer got out of prison and got his old job back working for Pharaoh; but then he forgot all about Joseph. Until, one day, Pharaoh had some weird dreams, and needed someone to help him figure them out. The cup bearer remembered Joseph, and told Pharaoh all about him. Pharaoh sent for Joseph and asked for his help.

Pharaoh told Joseph that he dreamt about a river. Then, he saw seven skinny cows come up out of the river and eat up seven fat cows. Whoa! That's way too weird. But what does it mean? Joseph prayed to God for wisdom, and God showed him the meaning of Pharaoh's dream.[22]

Joseph told Pharaoh that the fat cows meant there would be seven good years ahead when things would grow and there would be lots of food; but the skinny cows meant that at the end of those seven years, there would be a great famine when hardly anything would grow, and everyone would be really hungry.

Then, Joseph told pharaoh how to get around the problem. He told him to store up food when things are growing so that he would be able to help everyone when the famine arrived.

Wow, pharaoh was so grateful for the knowledge from God that he made Joseph second in charge of Egypt. Joseph was now in charge of lots of things, including getting people ready for the days ahead. So no more prison for Joseph. He got new clothes, servants, and a nice palace to live in!

In the years that followed, it happened just as God had said. There were seven awesome years in Egypt where they had plenty of food. They had pomegranates and dates and plums. They had camel's milk, and persimmons, and they had macadamia nuts and humus, grapes and olives. They had figs, lettuce and berries, and lots of bread to eat. They had pomelos and pigeons and pears. And they had walnuts.

Joseph saved up some of that food In a very big storehouse because he knew that the seven years of plenty would end, and seven lean years would follow, just as God showed pharaoh in the dream. And so it was as God said. Seven years later, the earth was very dry and very little food would grow. The animals had a hard time finding food, too. It was a very great famine. And the famine not only affected Egypt but most of the areas around Egypt. Even Joseph's family were having a hard time finding food.

* * * * * * *

A lot has happened in Joseph's family since his mean brothers sold him to the Ishmaelites. For one thing, Joseph had a new baby brother. Benjamin was born. Joseph didn't know about Benjamin because of the fact that he was taken away to Egypt.

One day, Joseph's brothers (not including Benjamin) decided to go Egypt to buy food; and after traveling for many days, the brothers arrived in Egypt. Boy, were they in for a surprise! They had no idea what God had done in Joseph's life;

that even though they hated Joseph, God loved him and was taking care of him. Do you remember all that God did for Joseph?

Let's go back in time and take another look. After Joseph's brothers threw him into a pit, God helped him to get out, and be carried away safely to Egypt by the Ishmaelite merchants. Then, He helped Joseph to get a job working for Potipher. After Joseph was thrown into prison, He helped him to get out and become ruler over all Egypt. God stayed with Joseph the entire time, through bad times and good times. You see, God had always intended for Joseph to be ruler over Egypt. All the while when it seemed like everything was going wrong for Joseph, God was in the background moving things along until finally, Joseph ended up right where He wanted him--in a great spot next to Pharaoh. That's going to be important because now Joseph has power to help a lot of people, including his family. But will he help his mean brothers? He has a lot of power now, so will he throw them into a dungeon, or feed them to the lions? Or will he will forgive them?

The big day comes and Joseph's brothers are in Egypt to buy food. Joseph sees a lot of people on a daily basis; that's his job—to distribute the food to those who need it. But one thing he never expected to see was his brothers walk into his palace and bow before him, asking for food.

It had been a really long time since they sold Joseph to the Ishmaelites, so they didn't recognize him. Here he was all grown up and living in a palace. But Joseph surely remembered them! He was so shocked to see them that it probably took him a minute to catch his breath. His heart was beating fast, and he couldn't help but stare at them.

When they told Joseph that they were in Egypt to buy grain, Joseph decided to heckle them a bit. "You are spies,"[23] Joseph said to his brothers. And his brothers got nervous and tried very hard to convince him that they were not spies. They told him about their father, Jacob, and that they had a little brother back home named Benjamin. Wow, that's another surprise! Joseph had no idea that he had a baby brother because he had been in Egypt the whole time.

"I have a little brother?" Joseph must have thought. He wanted very much to meet Benjamin, so he told his brothers that they would have to prove that they were not spies by bringing Benjamin to meet him. He would keep Simeon, one of the brothers, in prison, while the others go to get Benjamin.

The brothers went and got Benjamin and returned to Egypt. When they saw Joseph sitting on his throne, they bowed down to him again, out of respect (just as God had showed him in the dream.) They still didn't recognize Joseph and so Joseph pretended not to know them either. He asked about their father. "Is your father still living?"[24] He asked, because he really missed his Dad.

When Joseph saw Benjamin, "He asked, 'Is this your youngest brother, the one you told me about?'"[25] He was seeing Benjamin for the first time.

"Deeply moved at the sight of his brother, Joseph hurried out and looked for a place to weep."[26] He wanted to hug Benjamin. He wanted to sing and laugh and be happy; but he also remembered what his brothers did, how they hated him, and how they sold him into slavery. He hurried out of the room and found a place to sit alone and cry.

Then, he washed his face and tried to stay calm. He told his servants to serve the food, and he made sure Benjamin got a big serving, much more than his brothers.

As Joseph sat there and saw Benjamin and thought about all that happened, he couldn't control himself any longer. He yelled at his servants to leave his presence. And after his servants ran out of the room, Joseph wept in front of his brothers.

"I am Joseph!"[27] He said. His brothers just sat there in shock. No one wanted to eat anything at that moment. They probably felt their stomachs churning and wanted to pass out because it was all so sudden, and because they had been so mean to him. Now here he was with all the power in Egypt. Will he have his servants chop off their heads? They were "terrified at his presence."[28]

But there was no hatred in Joseph's heart. "'Come close to me...," he said, 'I am your brother, Joseph, the one you sold into Egypt!'"[29]

"Yeah, we know," they probably thought. "Please don't throw us to the lions." But Joseph didn't want revenge. He just wanted his family back. And so he said, "Do not be distressed and do not be angry with yourselves for selling me here, because it was to save lives that God sent me ahead of you."[30] Wow. In spite of all the crazy stuff that happened to him, Joseph could still see God at work. He could still see how God brought a lot of good out of it.

Joseph loved his brothers and so he tried to put the anger out of his heart, and the sadness of being away from his father, Jacob.

He felt the sadness, too, for not seeing Benjamin grow up—all those times they could have played together; he must have missed those. But, at least now, he has his family back.

Joseph spoke kindly to his brothers, and said, "I am your brother, Joseph, Come close to me." And they did. And he threw his arms around Benjamin and he wept. He kissed all his brothers and wept over them.

After Joseph hugged his brothers, he couldn't wait to see his Dad. When his Dad and brothers came to Egypt, to a place called Goshen, Joseph got into his chariot and drove to meet his Dad. "As soon as Joseph appeared before him, he threw his arms around his father and wept for a long time."[31]

Later on, Joseph took his sons to meet their grandpa Jacob. When Jacob saw them, he said, "I never expected to see you again, and now God has allowed me to see your children too."[32]

Wow. How awesome is that! God worked it all out!

* * * * * * *

When I finished writing the story of Joseph, I went for a walk in the Old City of Jerusalem. I thought about how God always works things out, and how much He cares about all that He created.

I felt like saying a special "thank you" to God, so I decided to walk to the Wailing Wall to pray. I walked past Uncle Heim's cafe, and took a left on a long road that led to the Wall. Then, there it was, like a mighty humongous mountain. I looked up. Whoa! The Wall seems to go all the way to Heaven.

I wondered if Joseph ever prayed at the Wall, and what he would have said to God; he would have had a lot of stuff to thank Him for.

Then, I thought about all the awesome things God does for me, and said, "Thank you, Father God for always working stuff out for me and for having a plan for my life." It wasn't all I wanted to say, but most of it got stuck inside my heart. I guess I just wanted Him to know that I love Him and that it meant a lot to me that He cares so much.

Then, it started to rain; lots of rain streaming down from Heaven, mixed with sunlight.

As I headed back home in the rain, I smiled, 'cause I think God heard me.

EXODUS.

MOSES
PRINCE of EGYPT

One day after dinner, Dad came into my room and sat beside me on my bed. "How are you doing, Sport?" he asked. Dad calls me "Sport" sometimes because we both love sports, like baseball and hockey.

"OK, Dad," I said. Then, I could tell he had something really important to tell me because he got quiet and looked down at the floor for a long time.

"I wanted to wait until you were old enough to tell you this, Davey, and yesterday you turned nine years old. I think it's time." I was a little nervous about what he had to say. Is he going to send me away like my friend Jonny's parents sent him away to school? He has to live there all the time and only gets to come home for Christmas. And if Dad and Mom weren't sending me away, maybe Dad got a new job and we might be moving away from my friends.

"I don't know how else to tell you this, Davey, so I will just say it," he said. "You are adopted." Then he kissed me on my forehead. Adopted? I had to think for a minute. What is he saying? Dad is not my real Dad and Mom is not my real Mom? "Do you have anything you want to say?" He asked.

"You're my second Dad?" I asked. "And Mom is my second Mom?"

"Yes."

"Where did my first Mom and Dad go?"

"I don't know, Davey, but they wanted you to have a good home so they gave you to us."

"Are they coming back?"

"No, Davey, they are not coming back."

"Are you sending me away to school?"

"School? Where did you get that idea?"

"Jonny's mom and dad sent him away to school and he only gets to come home at Christmas."

"We are certainly not sending you away. We want you here with us."

I didn't know why I felt like crying. I never cried except when my doggie, Simba, died. But that's how I felt inside, sort of sad. "You're always going to keep me?" I asked.

He picked me up and hugged me. "There is no way in the whole world that I would ever give you back!" he said.

And that's how I found out that my Dad is my second Dad. And my Mom is my second Mom. "Can I go sit in my boat?" I asked.

"Sure, Davey. Do you want me to go with you?"

"No. It's OK. I want to write with the dragon feather."

I have a rowboat in the solarium where I sit when I need time to think. So that's what I did. I got the dragon feather and paper and went out to the solarium with my two doggies, Chocolate Chip, and Mocha, and I sat in my boat and looked at the feather for a long time. At first, I had a hard time thinking of what to write about; then I remembered the story about Moses. He was adopted, too.

It's warm in the solarium, but it's snowing outside. Wow, snow in Jerusalem. It never snows here. It's really weird for ice to cover everything; but I'm glad it's Saturday and I don't have to go to school. So, I can just sit here in my boat and write about Moses.

I'm happy to get to the story about Moses because it takes place in Egypt; that's a place with lots of sun and sand, and it's really warm. I put the dragon feather on paper and try to imagine what it was like when Moses lived.

Suddenly, I see a sandstorm. And I see the sphinx and pyramids and the sky above Egypt is sort of orange yellow. And I hear a sound like, "Yaaaaawww!! Yaaawww!" Oh, wow. It's a camel, and he's walking across the sand with two guys; and the guys walk right in front of Pharaoh's palace. Let's go inside.

OK, OK, so this is what it looks like in here. Really cool, with papyrus plants in large clay pots near an open window. And the big guy is here, Pharaoh himself; he's sort of slouched over, sitting on his throne, and he looks worried. I mean, he's really scared about something, and I think I know what it is.

Remember Joseph? The guy with the coat of many colors. Well, he used to serve in this palace. He was second in command when he lived, and he served Pharaoh, but not this Pharaoh; it was a long time ago and they both died since then, and this new Pharaoh took over.

Joseph was pretty rich when he was alive and he took good care of his family, the Israelites, and since then, the Israelites grew and grew into a mighty nation, just as God had said they would. And that's why pharaoh is worried; he thinks that maybe the Israelites, also called, the Hebrews, will become super strong, side with his enemies, and take his country away from him. And that's when he decides to do some pretty bad things. First, he is going to make them into slaves. Why slaves? So that they feel tired and beat up and don't want to have any more kids. He wanted them to stop growing.

And that's what he did; he forced the Israelites to build large cities like Ramses and Pithom. But his plan didn't quite go as he hoped because the Israelites kept growing. So, he went back to thinking about other ways to cut down their size. That's when he made a really evil decision to kill many of the baby boys that belong to the Israelites.

This is the part of the story where we meet Moses.[33] He is a baby at the time and his Mom wants to save him from Pharaoh's crazy plan, so she made a special basket that could float in water like a boat, and she placed the baby in the basket, and then she placed the basket in the Nile River. She must have been really scared, but she had to do something to save Moses. So she told Miriam, his sister, to follow the basket and see where it ends up.

So there was the basket floating past the dragon flies and the tall papyrus grass, and past the water lilies and river rocks. It floated past the frogs and the fish swimming in the river. All the while, God was guiding the basket, until finally the basket came to a pool of water where Pharaoh's daughter was about to bathe. Suddenly, she heard the baby crying. Whaaaa! Whaaaa!

She looked around and looked around until she saw the basket, and when she looked inside the basket, wow, what is this? A cute little kid. She was so happy to find him that she said, wow, OK, I'm keeping him. When Miriam saw that Pharaoh's daughter found the baby, she went over to where they were and asked if she should go get someone to nurse the baby. Pharaoh's daughter said yes, and Miriam went and got the baby's Mommy. "Pharaoh's daughter said to her, 'Take this baby and nurse him for me, and I will pay you.' So the woman took the baby and nursed him. When the child grew older, she took him to Pharaoh's daughter and he became her son. She named him Moses..."[34]

So, even though Moses was an Israelite, he grew up like an Egyptian, with Pharaoh's daughter as his new Mommy. She was a princess, so that meant he was a prince of Egypt. He had lots of clothes, nice smelling stuff, and good food to eat. He had pomegranates, figs, and olives; and he had pita bread. He

had raisins, and grapes, and humus and peppermint; and he had pumpkin, corn, baby lettuce and pumpernickel seeds. But in all the cool stuff he had, he never forgot that he was an Israelite, a Hebrew. His second Mom must have told him that he was adopted because he grew up knowing who he was. He must have known that he was adopted.

One day Moses went for a walk because maybe he needed to get outside for some fresh air. While he was walking around, he saw something that made him mad—he saw an Egyptian slave master beating a Hebrew slave. He got so angry that he killed the Egyptian. Then he looked around because maybe he didn't mean to kill him, and when it looked like no one saw him, he dug a hole in the sand and buried the Egyptian's dead body.

The next day, he went back outside and saw two Hebrews fighting. He wanted everyone to get along so he said something like, "Hey, stop that." And when he did, one of the Hebrews turned to him and in a mean voice, he said, "Are you thinking of killing me as you killed the Egyptian?"[35] Now Moses knew that they saw what he did. He knew, too, that Pharaoh would be really mad at him, so he ran away to a place called Midian.

One day, while living in Midian, Moses looked towards a place called Mt. Horeb and saw a fire on the mountain. Hey, what's going on there? So he went to check it out. Then, he saw something surprising: a bush was burning but not burning up. How is that possible? Then, he heard a Voice coming from the fire! It was the powerful voice of God, and He said, "I am the God of your father, the God of Abraham, the God of Isaac and the God of Jacob."[36]

Wow, the God of Abraham! Wow. Wow. Wow. Wow! Moses had heard about Him from his family, as all Israelites did, now He was speaking to him. How amazing was that!!

"At this, Moses hid his face, because he was afraid to look at God."[37] The Lord said, "I have indeed seen the misery of my people in Egypt. I have heard them crying out because of their slave drivers, and I am concerned about their suffering. So I have come down to rescue them from the hand of the Egyptians and to bring them up out of that land into a good and spacious land, a land flowing with milk and honey..."[3] So you see, God didn't forget about His people, the Israelites. He saw their suffering. He saw that Pharoah was really mean to them. God said to Moses, "So now, go. I am sending you to Pharaoh to bring my people the Israelites out of Egypt."[39]

"But Moses said to God, 'Who am I, that I should go to Pharaoh and bring the Israelites out of Egypt?'"[40] Moses wasn't in a hurry to go back to Egypt. First, he had killed someone and buried him in the sand. And also, Pharaoh was mad at him for doing that. Plus, he sometimes stuttered. The words didn't always come out right when he spoke. Moses asked God to please send someone else. But God saw something in Moses. He believed Moses was the perfect person to speak to Pharaoh. When Moses kept giving excuses, God got really angry at him and decided to send his brother Aaron along with him. Moses was still scared, so "God said, 'I will be with you...'"[41]

God is awesome and can make Himself invisible and so even though Moses and Aaron wouldn't be able to see Him, He will be with them to help them. So, you see, Moses will have a lot of power with him when he goes to see Pharaoh.

* * * * * *

The big day arrives and Moses and Aaron are in Egypt to speak to Pharaoh. Boy, Moses must have been super nervous, but he felt better knowing God was with Him. So, he walks into Pharaoh's throne room with his brother Aaron; then he walks up to Pharaoh's throne.

When Moses tells Pharaoh why he came to see him, Pharaoh is not too happy. Moses said, "This is what the Lord, the God of Israel, says: 'Let my people go...'"[42] Pharaoh got real angry at Moses, and took it out on the Hebrew slaves; he told the slave masters that they should make it double hard for the slaves by giving them extra work to do.

When Moses saw how Pharaoh made life harder for the Israelites, he kind of feels like giving up, and goes to talk to God. "Then the Lord said to Moses, 'Go, tell Pharaoh king of Egypt to let the Israelites go out of his country.'"[43] So that's what Moses does. He walks back into the palace, and walks up to Pharaoh and told him what God said. Pharaoh is given a second chance to set things right; but still, he refuses to let the Israelites go free from slavery, so God decides that it's time to send the plagues!

"The Lord said to Moses, 'Tell Aaron, take your staff and stretch out your hand over the waters of Egypt--over the streams and canals, over the ponds and all the reservoirs--and they will turn to blood. Blood will be everywhere in Egypt, even in vessels of wood and stone.'"[44]

And it was amazing!! Aaron stretched his hand over the waters of Egypt, and whoa!! The clear fresh streams of water turned to blood. The water in the stone

jars turned to blood, too. But Pharaoh's heart became hardened; that means he still would not listen to God. And he still would not listen to Moses and Aaron. So, there will be many more plagues!!

"Then the Lord said to Moses, 'Tell Aaron, 'Stretch out your hand with your staff over the streams and canals and ponds, and make frogs come up on the land of Egypt. So Aaron stretched out his hand over the waters of Egypt, and the frogs came up and covered the land."[45] Hundreds and hundreds of frogs just kept coming out of the streams and river canals. And you know what, for a while, it looked like the plague worked.

Well, I kind of like frogs, but Pharaoh hated them, and so he sent for Moses and Aaron and said, "Pray to the Lord to take the frogs away from me and my people, and I will let your people go..."[46]

"After Moses and Aaron left Pharaoh, Moses cried out to the Lord about the frogs he had brought on Pharaoh. And the Lord did what Moses asked. The frogs died in the houses, in the courtyards and in the fields."[47]

"But when Pharaoh saw that there was relief, he hardened his heart and would not listen to Moses and Aaron, just as the Lord had said."[48] So, there would be another plague. This next plague would fall from the sky.

God sent a windy icy rain storm to Egypt. Whoa. Chunks of ice fell from the sky and broke a lot of stuff. God was trying to tell Pharaoh something like, listen, you can't just keep My people because you feel like it; and you can't go around making them slaves. You have to let them go out of your country. But Pharoah wouldn't listen to God, so that's why He sent the ice storm.

When the rain and hail and thunder stopped, Pharaoh hardened his heart; that means he still wouldn't listen to God, so God asked Pharaoh, "How long will you refuse to humble yourself before Me? Let My people go so that they may worship Me."[49] Pharaoh was super-stubborn, so there would be another plague. This time, grasshoppers will cover the land of Egypt.

"Moses stretched out his staff over Egypt,"[50] and God sent a wind from the East that blew across Egypt for a whole day and a whole night. And when the Egyptians looked outside the next day, they saw lots and lots of grasshoppers that came in on the wind. The grasshoppers were everywhere, and they would ruin whatever was left in Egypt; so Pharaoh sent for Aaron and Moses.

* * * * * * *

When Moses and Aaron went back to Pharaoh, he thought about letting the men go to the desert to worship God, but didn't want the women, kids, and animals to go. That wasn't going to work for Moses, so he said everyone would have to go. Pharaoh got angry. No! He said to Moses and Aaron. "Have only the men go."[51] Then he had Moses and Aaron thrown out of his palace.

Pharaoh is super stubborn, but God will not back down. Before it's all over, He will send a total of ten plagues to Egypt. Each one will be tougher than the last one.

This time, darkness will cover the land of Egypt. This wasn't just regular darkness, it was darkness the Egyptians could feel; like the darkness in a chimney at night when the fire is out, or the darkness under the bed in old empty houses. It was dark-darkness.

"Total darkness covered all Egypt for three days."[52] The sky gave no light and all of Egypt was so dark that they couldn't even see each other. They couldn't see the windows. They couldn't see the doors to go outside. They couldn't see their hands or their toes. It was very dark for three days. But, guess what, all of God's people had light where they lived. Isn't that awesome? The darkness didn't bother God's people at all. They had plenty of light. God took care of them!

After three days of stumbling around in the dark and bumping into stuff, Pharaoh was ready to let God's people go. "Then Pharaoh summoned Moses and said, 'Go, worship the Lord and even your women and children may go with you; only leave your flocks and herds behind.'"[53]

Moses told pharaoh that the animals must go with them as well because some of them would be used as a sacrifice to God. That made Pharaoh really angry. "Pharaoh said to Moses, 'Get out of my sight! Make sure you do not appear before me again! The day you see my face you will die.'"[54]

"'Just as you say,' Moses replied, 'I will never appear before you again.'"[55] Moses would never again have to appear before Pharaoh, which was great news for Moses, but bad news for Pharaoh; because now, God will deal with Pharaoh Himself. God will visit Egypt with the final plague. He will pass through Egypt at midnight and at that time, all the firstborn males in Egypt would die, even the firstborn of the cattle. But it would not be so among the Israelites. All their firstborns would live. They were trusting God and they were His people; they were part of His Kingdom. And He kept them safe.

Once Pharaoh saw that a lot of people had died because he kept the Israelites as slaves, he decided to let God's people go, including their animals.

So all the Israelites got their stuff together and headed out of Egypt! There was probably one million people in all, with camels, and carts, lots of straw, and water pouches, bowls with persimmons, pomegranates and plums, bags of rice, dates, figs, and humus with pita bread. A lot of people and a lot of food for the journey through the desert. But where were all these people going? To the land God had promised them; to Canaan, a place of milk and honey and green trees, and olives, and grass, and plums.

****

As they head through the desert, some of the Israelites look super happy and some look a little scared. And God is with them to help them. He is traveling in a super-awesome pillar of cloud in the sky and leading them towards Canaan. Also, a mighty Angel of God is traveling in front of the Israelites. Lots of power surrounds the Israelites as they walk towards Canaan, to keep them safe!

But, shortly after the Israelites left Egypt, Pharaoh is sitting around thinking, and says, "What have we done?"[56] Now, he doesn't have any Israeli slaves to push around, so, he changes his mind and goes after them with his army!

While the Israelites are tired and standing in front of the Red Sea, suddenly, Pharaoh and his army appear in the distance, kicking up a bunch of sand, rushing towards them; and he looks pretty mean and angry!

The Israelites get scared because they are in front of the Red Sea with no where to hide, and they feel trapped! They think Pharaoh is about to swoop down and capture them and force them to go back to Egypt, or maybe even kill them; so they cry out to Moses! "What have you done to us by bringing us out of Egypt?"[57] Moses is a little scared too, but he tells the people, "The Lord will fight for you; you need only to be still."[58]

Then, God speaks to Moses in a strong and powerful voice and says, "Raise your staff and stretch out your hand over the sea to divide the water so that the Israelites can go through the sea on dry ground."[59]

Moses is like, OK, let's go guys, and he raises his staff and stretches it over the sea. Wow. Guess what; as Moses stretched his hand over the sea, God sent a great wind from the east and that great wind drove the sea back. Swoosh, the water rose up on the left side and, Swoosh, the water rose up on the right side, and there was dry land in the middle. Everybody go!! Go, go, go!!!

And the Israelites, all one million of them, start across the sea-bed. The kids, the grandparents, the goats, the mommies, and all the wagons with pita bread and herbs, all making their way across on dry land. Awesome!! Meanwhile, God and His angel break formation, and both of them go to the back of the Israeli camp.

God is traveling in an awesome pillar of cloud. He's looking at the Egyptian army, then, Kapowey! He sends darkness in front of them so they couldn't see how to move. And guess what. He puts light around the Israeli camp. Whoa. Awesome! This all looks great from space, with darkness on one side of the great cloud and light on the other. God is giving the Israelites time to make it through the sea, and He wants them to have plenty of light.

As the Israelites make it to the other side of the sea bed, the darkness lifts and the Egyptians can see again. Whoa! What's going on? They see the water heaped on both sides and all the Israelites going across to the other side. Pharaoh said something like, "Hey guys, let's go get them!" And they run after the Israelites.

"Then the Lord said to Moses, 'Stretch out your hand over the sea so that the waters may flow back over the Egyptians and their chariots and horsemen.'"[60] So, "Moses stretched out his hand over the sea, and...the sea went back to its place. The Egyptians were fleeing toward it, and the Lord swept them into the sea."[61]

"That day the Lord saved Israel from the hands of the Egyptians...And when the Israelites saw the great power the Lord displayed against the Egyptians, the people feared the Lord and put their trust in Him and in Moses His servant."[62]

So that's how it happened. God showed up and saved His people and we see that He has super-powers, and no one can match it! Pharaoh tried and look what happened to him. Those who trust God have a great future because He is a mighty King. And an awesome Friend!!

* * * * * * *

When I finished writing the Bible stories, I got up and went outside. Wow, look up. Can you see it, too? There, high in the sky, is the Milky Way galaxy, and the Horseshoe Nebulae. All the world that God created for miles and miles and miles. I take a deep breath and I feel so happy that I am part of the great world that God created. He created me and Mom and Dad and both my doggies, Mocha, and Chocolate Chip.

And He created my llama goat and all my fingers and toes; and He created grasshoppers and hugs and lollipops and lakes and all the fish in the sea. He created anemone and whales and fish that fly, and all the dolphins and the sea horse, too. And He made persimmons, the sea eagle, and dinosaurs. Wow. He created all of that because He loves me. And because He loves you, too.

* * * * * * *

While I was looking up at the sky and thinking about all God created, my Dad walked out of the house and stood next to me.

"I did it, Dad." I said. "I wrote some stories with the dragon feather."

"Wow, Davey, you finished some of the stories?"

"Yes, Dad. Do you think God likes the way I wrote them?"

"Well, why don't you close your eyes and ask Him?" And so that's what I did. When I opened my eyes, Dad was smiling.

"You heard," I said, smiling.

Dad kissed my forehead and took my hand in his. Now, we get to celebrate, Davey. Let's go to the solarium and have the biggest cup of hot chocolate in the whole world.

"Yeah!!" I said. But as we were walking to the solarium I looked up at the sky. "Please come too," I said to God. I wanted Him to know that I love Him with my whole heart; and I wanted Him to sit next to me when I had my hot chocolate. He's awesome and kind and I wanted to sit next to Him when I had my hot chocolate.

THE GOSPEL

God loves us, so He sent His Son, Jesus the Christ, also known as Yeshua, to die for our sins. Now, we don't have to die for our sins. The Bible promises: "If you declare with your mouth, 'Jesus is Lord,' and believe in your heart that God raised him from the dead, you will be saved." (Romans 10:9)

PRAYER OF SALVATION

I confess with my mouth that Jesus is Lord. And I believe in my heart that God raised Him from the dead.
Now, Lord Jesus, forgive me for my sins.
I accept you as my lord and savior. Come into my heart and make me over in your image. Thank You, Lord.

Dr. Delcie Palmer, JD is the second great grand daughter of Paul Bogle, the revolutionary whose image is found on Jamaican currency. And if anything, she inherited his love for Christ and his passion for positive world change. She is a graduate of the University of Massachusetts School of Law at Dartmouth, Harvard University DCE (communications), and Lesley University (healing modalities/counseling).

Author of "Courageous, A Trailblazer's Journey to the Far Side of the World," and the "Davey and the Dragon Feather" series, she brings whimsy and warmth to every story with the simple goal of inspiring faith in God and instilling courage.

Other Books by the Author

Available at faithbridgecafe.com,
Amazon.com,
and wherever books are sold.

ENDNOTES

1	Genesis 1:3, NKJV	37	Exodus 3:6, NIV
2	Genesis 1:9, NKJV	38	Exodus 3:7-8, NIV
3	Genesis 1:29, NKJV	39	Exodus 3:10, NIV
4	Genesis 1:26, NKJV	40	Exodus 3:11, NIV
5	Genesis 1:27-28, NKJV	41	Exodus 3:12, NIV
6	See Genesis 3, NKJV	42	Exodus 5:1, NIV
7	See Genesis 3, NKJV	43	Exodus 6:10, NIV
8	See Genesis 3, NKJV	44	Exodus 7:19, NIV
9	See Genesis 3 NKJV	45	Exodus 8: 5-6, NIV
10	See Genesis 3, NKJV	46	Exodus 8:8, NIV
11	See Genesis 3, NIV	47	Exodus 8:12-13, NIV
12	See Genesis 3:15, NKJV	48	Exodus 8:15, NIV
13	Genesis 6: 12-13, NKJV	49	Exodus 10:3, NIV
14	See Genesis 6:20	50	Exodus 10:13, NIV
15	See Genesis 6:9-12 NIV	51	Exodus 10:11, NIV
16	See Genesis 9:16, NKJV	52	Exodus 10:22, NIV
17	See Genesis 37:18, NKJV	53	Exodus 10:24, NIV
18	See Genesis 37:33	54	Exodus 10:28, NIV
19	See Genesis 37:33	55	Exodus 10:29, NIV
20	See Genesis 39:7-20	56	Exodus 14:5, NIV
21	Genesis 39:20-21, NKJV	57	Exodus 14:11, NIV
22	See Genesis 41	58	Exodus 14:13, NIV
23	Genesis 42:9, NKJV	69	Exodus 14:16, NIV
24	Genesis 43:7, NKJV	60	Exodus 14:26, NIV
25	Genesis 43:29, NKJV	61	Exodus 14:27, NIV
26	Genesis 43:30, NKJV	62	Exodus 14:30-31, NIV
27	Genesis 45:3, NKJV		
28	Genesis 45:3, NKJV		
29	Genesis 45:2-3, NKJV		
30	Genesis 45:5, NKJV		
31	Genesis 48:29, NKJV		
32	Genesis 48:11, NIV		
33	See Exodus 2		
34	Exodus 2:9-10, NIV		
35	Exodus 2:11-14, NIV		
36	Exodus 3:6, NIV		

"Archaeopteryx," Wikipedia, accessed 4/27/24, https://en.wikipedia.org/wiki/Archaeopterayyx

DISCLAIMER

The Davey and the Dragon Feather series of books are for educational and entertainment purposes only. Davey is a fictional character inspired by the valor and faith of King David of the Holy Scriptures. Although the backstory of the Davey character is fictional, the Bible stories and Scripture quotations in the Davey Series of books are NOT fiction. (Some descriptive deatils were added by the author in scene development).. The Holy Scriptures demonstrate the amazing love and devotion of God to His people, and His people's love for Him.

Davey pens his stories using a rare "Dragon Feather," inspired by the Archaeopteryx dinosaur bird which some believe lived in the "Late Jurasic Period."

God loves you and wants to hear from you.
Feel free to use the following pages for your special prayers.

PRAYER PAGES

_____

_____

_____

_____

_____

_____